in the same series

lofts, a style of living, élodie piveteau - caroline wietzel
cabins, dens and bolt-holes, frank roots
graffiti, sandrine pereira

Translation by Translate-A-Book, Oxford

Design and creation: GRAPH'M/Nord Compo, France

ISBN: 2-7528-0216-1
Publisher code: T00216

Copyright registration: October 2005
Printed in Italy by Rotolito Lombarda

www.fitwaypublishing.com

Fitway Publishing
Fitway Publishing – 12, avenue d'Italie – 75627 Paris cedex 13, France

archiDesign

spas

katya pellegrino

fitway.
publishing

contents

ocean oases

Everything there is harmony and beauty,
luxury, calm and delight

The celebrated French poet Charles Baudelaire wrote these lines over a century and a half ago in one of his best-known poems, *The Invitation to the Voyage*. Had he been privileged to pen a preface to the present volume, he would doubtless have been tempted to repeat those selfsame sentiments:

Everything there is harmony and beauty, luxury, calm and delight.

What could be more apposite to describe this invitation to a voyage that encompasses upwards of thirty of the world's most extraordinary spa resorts scattered around the globe in major cities, on faraway islands, in mountain retreats or in desert oases?

Each double-page spread in the remarkable selection that follows portrays a hedonistic universe of well-being and elegance. The author describes each spa retreat in colourful detail, focusing on the unique geographical location, architecture, interior design features and treatment facilities that combine to make it a unique haven of luxury and tranquillity. Beauty is the watchword here – that sense of inner peace that descends when piloting a canoe at dawn in some upper reach of the Amazon or lying on a secluded beach, gazing at a night sky festooned with stars.

In each resort, the guest reigns supreme, pampered at every turn; each siesta and each massage a further milestone on the road to inner peace. Sun, water, rare essences, exotic perfumes and a delicious silence are the common denominator, irrespective of whether the resort in question is in India, South Africa, the Seychelles or in the very heart of downtown New York City. Everyday cares and stresses are soothed away as the hectic pace of contemporary urban life slows to a standstill.

Spa living is luxury at its most refined. And there can scarcely be a better way to anticipate it than by turning the pages of this beautifully crafted and superbly illustrated invitation to a voyage unlike any other …

The editor

city sanctuaries

Four Seasons Hotel George V Paris
France

The flamboyantly *art déco* Four Seasons Hotel George V is no mere monument to the historical splendours of Paris past and present, it is a benchmark of modernity.

The hotel lobby sets the tone. Magnificent flower arrangements by the ultra-talented Jeff Letham, a former male model who has turned his hand to the art of floral design, frame the entrance to the prestigious three-star restaurant, *Le Cinq*, and add to the unique sense of studied harmony and tranquillity that pervades the foyer and the bar area.

The hotel's imposing corridors, the immense rooms and apartments are a throwback to a bygone age of opulence and refinement. Carefully selected antiques, discreet *objets d'art* and tasteful soft furnishings combine to create a sense of luxury that is welcoming but carefully understated. Top interior designer Pierre-Yves Rochon has decorated the George V Spa as he might have a Parisian *salon* or *boudoir*. Muted natural colours exude taste and elegance. The walls are hung with works of art. Chairs and sofas are upholstered in tapestry fabrics by Jouy. An intangible fragrance of essential oils permeates the air and instils a sense of well-being, encouraging guests to indulge in the sensual delights of the signature Deep Chocolate Treatment, an experience that brings back delicious aromas of childhood.

The Four Seasons George V Spa escalates the art of service to fresh heights, meeting the expectations of its guests with an unostentatious display of excellence.

Four Seasons Hotel Ritz Lisbon
Portugal

The Four Seasons Hotel Ritz, set on the edge of the Edward VII Gardens, is reminiscent of the finest *grand cru*: it reveals its character and quality only to those willing to savour it.

The Ritz is the figurehead and *nec plus ultra* of Lisbon's hotels, the Mecca of modernity of the Portuguese capital, notwithstanding its Louis XVI and *art déco* rooms, lounges and restaurants with their inimitable blend of space, light and perspective. The Ritz Spa, by contrast, is totally and invitingly Zen. It is approached along corridors decorated with abstract paintings and bronze sculptures. The pool area continues this Oriental minimalist theme, inducing a feeling of spiritual well-being. Restful sandalwood, cinnamon and eucalyptus fragrances fill the air. Underfoot, heated limestone floors gently massage the feet. The walls are tiled in polished stone. Papyrus, Indian bamboo and loofah gourds are discreetly displayed. The spa guest is ushered in to a cubicle replete with Eastern promise. A gentle mist of jasmine, citrus fruits, green tea and soft, soothing voices.

The Holistic Back, Face and Scalp Massage Treatment is a subtle blend of the natural and the mystical, addressing each of the senses together and in turn. Exotic essences, gentle hands and the soft murmur of Oriental incantations to the accompaniment of gentle background music combine to generate a plethora of sensations.

Gran Hotel La Florida
Barcelona, Spain

Barcelona the Beautiful. The Catalan capital has re-invented itself since the 1990s, developing a kind of everyday 'street art' that also permeates the Gran Hotel La Florida, a jewel of a hotel nestling high up on the Tibidado mountain only seven kilometres from downtown Barcelona. The Gran Hotel La Florida looks down on the myriad lights of the metropolis spread out below, like a canvas painted by Matisse. The hotel has recently been refurbished and classified as a historic monument. It now offers a singular blend of contemporary art and design, with classic touches and original features that complement and intensify its dramatic location.

Each of La Florida's eight suites has been decorated by a leading artist – and each exhibits the innovative sense of creativity so typical of Barcelona. Ceilings are painted iridescent silver, geometrical friezes adorn the walls, folded white paper lamps and luminous globes cast spirals of light, and a Ben Jakob-designed twenty-seven metre-high fibre-optic cone in one corner of the foyer ascends vertiginously to the top floor of the hotel.

The Zen Zone Spa exhibits the same symbiotic properties. The basic tonalities are greys and reds. A glass-walled, L-shaped indoor-outdoor infinity pool is a curtain of falling rain. The natural light enchants and dazzles the guest, who can scarcely believe this level of sophistication can be created by such apparently simple means.

The Zen Zone Massage is the signature treatment here. It is accompanied by candlelight and a backdrop of serene incantation. Nimble yet firm hands knead a willing body, massaging lightly or forcefully as required, developing a balanced choreography that builds to a ninety-minute sequence culminating in total and complete relaxation. And, as the sun sets and the sky darkens, there is still time to sit on the private hotel terrace and savour yet another moment of pure enchantment.

Ksar Char-Bagh
Marrakech, Morocco

Water is the keynote at Ksar Char-Bagh: water inside, water outside in the palace gardens, water trickling through sand, water coursing through the *seguiat* conduits of the medieval herb garden, water in pools and fountains.

It took several years and the combined talents of a dedicated French couple, Nicole and Patrick Grandsire-Levillair, to conjure from virtually nothing the Ksar Char-Bagh Palace, which lies in the La Palmeraie (palm grove) region of Marrakech. The hotel has a centuries-old patina, its graceful arabesques and crenellated towers reflected in the waters of an oasis garden fringed by bigaroon cherry and slender spindle trees.

Nicole designed this palace of dreams from plans and drawings of 14th-century Moorish palaces, determined from the outset to achieve simplicity and moderation rather than give in to excess. The end result lives up to her expectations: Ksar Char-Bagh is now a discreet and harmonious amalgam of Syrian furnishings, silks, tented ceilings and restrained arabesque stucco work.

The palace boasts areas with evocative names such as the Courtyard of the Gueizas, the Passage of the Falcons, the Corridor of Carpets, or the Galleries of the Muqarnas. This *Arabian Nights* theme is continued into the Harim Suites, each of which has a terrace or private garden and features wall niches and high, vaulted ceilings, with floors tiled in beige or grey marble, walls clad in tinted whitewash (*tadelak*t) and bathrooms with sarcophagus-like baths.

Come sundown, it is time to luxuriate in a sunken bath filled with essential oils and orange blossom, and to gaze through the *mashrabiya* window towards the oasis garden beyond. Alternatively, one can opt for an argan-oil massage, either under white skeins of sari cloth in an open-air room clad in ochre-coloured limestone or indoors, in a lamp-lit room furnished with oriental rugs and scatter cushions. The eloquent simplicity of the *hammam* steam bath is also tempting; here, skilled Moroccan masseurs are on hand to practise their centuries-old skills, starting with that all-important rubdown. The steam bath, an octagonal tub in chocolate-coloured veined marble, is straight out of the *Arabian Nights*, an atmosphere compounded by fragrant, flickering candles.

By starlight and by candlelight, Ksar Char-Bagh is an exquisite distillation of perfume and pleasure. The mind wanders off into a world of its own, conjuring dreams of bygone sultans and caliphs.

Mandarin Oriental Hyde Park
London, United Kingdom

Kensington is the epitomy of the best of London. West Kensington has its own charm, whereas the stately Victorian houses of South Kensington, particularly Knightsbridge, boast stone steps, carved and gilded columns, pink and red marble-tiled hallways, and log fires.

This is the setting for the Mandarin Oriental Hyde Park, a haven of quiet courtesy and Victorian decorum. Grained marble and granite, stucco and arches abound in this refined hotel. The *fin-de-siècle* elegance of the bedrooms, with their muted lighting, soft cream fabrics, four-poster beds and antique ornaments, offers an antidote to the stresses of everyday urban life,

In the Mandarin Oriental Spa a different atmosphere reigns. The guest enters a neutral-toned world of granite, with unobtrusive wooden panelling and glass fixtures. In the spa proper, the fragrance of eucalyptus, the muted sound of running water and delicate pipe melodies tempt

the guest into the hands of the therapist. Ayurvedic Holistic Body Treatment is highly recommended. The guest is led to a plain cubicle where the eyes relax and the mind seems to float like a feather on the surface of a stream. The procedure is explained: the feet are cleansed, then there is a choice of exfoliation and invigorating massage using exotic oils and lotions. A pleasant sensation of drowsiness sets in. In the background, a gong is struck lightly to ward off evil spirits.

Mandarin Oriental
New York, United States

The brand-new Mandarin Oriental teeters high above Columbus Circle between the 35th and 54th floors of the Time Warner Center and affords unparalleled views over Central Park and the towering skyscrapers of New York.

The Big Apple is a churning cauldron of ethnic and cultural diversity, a city of extremes. On the other hand, the Mandarin Oriental is an oasis of urban calm. Its bedrooms and suites are designed in a sophisticated and glamorous oriental style, credit for which must go to designer Tony Chi (of ultra-chic Mobar fame). The 207 metre-square Presidential Suite is the Mandarin's crowning glory – and,

incidentally, reputed to be the most expensive hotel suite in the entire United States.

The Mandarin Spa Suite is the ultimate destination for those who wish to flee the stress of urban life. Nothing could be farther from the madding crowd. And nothing is calculated to put a guest more at ease than the Spa's 'Time Rituals', personalised treatments that encompass all the senses. Bamboo floors, natural stone, therapeutic colours, Chinese furnishings and Japanese rice paper complement the Mandarin Oriental's overall architectonic and interior design features and immediately induce a sense of harmony and peace.

The time-honoured rituals involve a plant-extract massage accompanied by Tibetan chimes to cleanse and purify mind and body, followed by a comprehensive assault on the five senses using essential oils, chromotherapy, infusions, soft chanting and pain-free exfoliation. The entire treatment lasts about one and a half hours, after which the guest feels at peace with the world and, in some strange way, *different*.

Outside, the New York nightlife beckons and the eye is inexorably drawn to the thousand and one stars that symbolise the pulsating energy of this vibrant city.

La Réserve
Geneva, Switzerland

La Réserve is located in the heart of a landscaped park on the shores of Lake Geneva. Entering the lobby of this red-brick building with its subtle juxtaposition of texture and colour represents the first step on a voyage of discovery. Parrots fashioned from variegated resins are perched on lamps. Butterfly collections adorn the walls. And the eye is drawn to the life-size baby elephant figures and the lion's feet console tables.

La Réserve owes its unique ambience to the talented Jacques Garcia, whose choice of styles and colours imparts an unmistakable intimacy. The interplay of colours, objects and soft furnishings is a triumphant blend of modernism and safari-style exoticism.

The bedrooms also reflect this 'contemporary colonial' approach: oiled chestnut-wood floors, velour plaid throws, and wine-coloured, caramel, ivory or celadon green taffeta curtains, depending on the colour scheme of the room. Headboards are fashioned from woven leather thongs, bookshelves are in dark wood, and the cabin-trunk consoles are padded with ox-blood leather. A total change from day-to-day surroundings.

The 2,000 metre-square La Réserve Spa explores the theme of travel to another world. It has been christened 'Une Autre Histoire' and that is precisely what it is, 'a different matter entirely', with echoes of Jules Verne's *Twenty Thousand Leagues Under the Sea*. Immaculate fabrics screen off relaxation areas, not least a very attractive bar with half-baby urchin, half-jellyfish lamps and white-leather Mediterranean-style sofas.

The seventeen treatment rooms give off a sensual yet understated fragrance of sandalwood and other aromatic oils. The name for each cubicle reinforces the sense of the exotic and the underlying theme of escapism – 'Awakening the Senses', 'Oriental Dreams', and so on. It is here that La Réserve's signature treatment, Chinese Tui-Na massage, is proposed.

Guests searching for a new sensory experience would be well advised to follow the 'Siamese Ritual', where silk-soft hands gently massage the body and exfoliation is followed by the application of coconut oils and puréed papaya. This age-old ritual has a predictably calming and restorative effect on mind and body.

The Setai
Miami South Beach, United States

The long ribbon of white sand and powdered shell is fringed by palm trees. The air is marshmallow-light. This is Miami: Ocean Drive in South Beach.

The South Beach section of Miami dates back to the 1930s and the hotels here are fortress-like affairs, their resolutely geometrical façades punctuated by porthole windows in emulation of the luxury cruise liners of years gone by. The former Dempsey Vanderbilt Hotel opened its doors in 1938; it has now been transformed into The Setai, a meticulously replicated eight-storey *art déco* landmark building that backs on to a forty-storey glass tower.

The Setai stands out among its competitors on account of its resolutely contemporary look, pure lines and ultra-minimalist decoration – a tribute to the skills of trailblazing designers Jean Michel Gathy and Jaya Ibrahim. The Setai's *art déco* origins are at their most evident in the foyer but, here too, the distinctive oriental tradition of elegant simplicity is sustained via Chinese vases, sculptures and artworks, including some splendid bronzes from Shanghai. The bedrooms and suites bear all the hallmarks of made-to-measure design, with soft furnishings in wild silk, black granite floors and teak furniture. This strikingly original decor is carried over into the crisp lines of the inviting champagne, caviar and shellfish bar.

The Asian theme is at its most pronounced in the Setai Spa. Here, the mood is mellow and one hundred per cent Zen, perfect therapy for typically stressed-out New Yorkers. There are no fewer than three magnificent sky-blue plunge pools of varying depths.

The philosophy underpinning the Setai Spa is derived from ancient Sanskrit legend that relates the quest embarked upon by Hindu deities to discover a natural elixir of immortality and eternal youth. The Spa makes no such claims, but it does propose treatments dedicated to restoring the mind, the body and the soul. All the rituals and applications are in the capable hands of Balinese therapists.

The signature Marma Massage entails stimulating the flow of energy to promote harmony of body and mind. The massage engenders virtually total relaxation and a most agreeable sensation of contentment and pleasure.

In the evenings, take a stroll along Ocean Drive, listen to the muted sounds of the Atlantic Ocean and, if you're in the mood for it, yield to the temptations of switched-on Miami nightlife.

rural retreats

Les Barmes de l'Ours
Val-d'Isère, France

Bourg-Saint-Maurice is at the end of the line and everyone gets off here. A narrow road skirts the lake, then plunges into the rock face, emerging from a final tunnel 1,850 metres up the mountainside at Val-d'Isère in the region known as the Haute-Tarentaise.

Val-d'Isère: birthplace of ski legend Jean-Claude Killy and home to the Les Barmes de l'Ours Hotel. The hotel takes its name from the rock escarpment where brown bears used to hibernate or take refuge during a storm. The choice of name is apt: Les Barmes de l'Ours is a refuge – and a delight.

A mantle of snow has descended on this Savoyard chalet with its welcoming stone and larchwood entrance, but guests are soon cocooned in bedrooms and suites that mix contemporary elegance and cosy rusticity. On the first floor, the overall 'feel' is decidedly Nordic, an impression reinforced by the whitewashed walls and waxed woodwork. One floor further up, the mood shifts and the decor takes on more than a hint of Old England, all leather and tartan and deep-pile carpets. The next floor is unashamedly 'Alpine', with typical Savoyard furniture. The fourth floor is spacious and contemporary. And the fifth and top floor is given over to modern suites decorated in a rich range of colours, from dark blue and mauve to chocolate and zebra-stripe motifs.

The Spa is a blue-grey cameo of marble from the quarries at Villette. The glass-walled pool mirrors the dazzling light reflected from the snow outside. White-upholstered *chaise longues* are arranged on a rostrum of light-toned wood that adds a touch of warmth. The window-wall affords an astonishing vista of the mountain peaks that ring the resort – the Solaise and the Tsanteleina among the most spectacular.

Spa treatment at Les Barmes de l'Ours is geared towards winter sports. Expert hands release tensions in a body tightened by the exertions of a day on the slopes. Essential oils and potions are gently applied to faces scorched by the Alpine sun. Tired skin absorbs and responds to a thorough facial, then it's off to the steam bath to soothe away any lingering aches and pains.

At sunset, an early evening stroll in the crystalline air is a definite *must*.

Begawan Giri Estate
Bali, Indonesia

Discreetly tucked away amid tropical vines, towering bamboo trees and wild coffee shrubs in the heart of the Balinese jungle in the Indonesian archipelago are several luxurious *feng-shui*-inspired bungalows: the Begawan Giri Estate.

The exotic decor is in tune with this natural setting. The 'Bayugita' Pavilion has a post-colonial feel, with floors in Javanese teak and ceilings woven from coconut fibre; the 'Tirta Ening' is all Zen and water features; and the 'Wanakasa' is an ecologically correct treehouse communing with the surrounding jungle. Elegant touches abound in the judicious use of wood and stone and the careful but casual distribution of precious objects both ancient and modern. Spacious terraces are shaded by a jungle canopy teeming with birds and other wildlife and look out over rice paddies tipped with green shoots. In the distance, the eye is drawn to the graceful undulations of the jungle vegetation and the perennial gurgling waters of the Ayung river. It gets hot here – very hot – but the suites each have that vital luxury, a private swimming pool.

rural retreats

The Shambhala Spa is redolent of exotic plants and flowers, as one might hope in such inviting surroundings. Treatment is traditionally provided out in the open, to the sound of running water in the natural pools dotted around the estate and from the Begawan Giri's own natural freshwater spring.

The signature treatment at the estate is the legendary Javanese Mandi Lulur, a ritual practised in the royal palaces of Java since the 17th century and handed down from generation to generation. Essences of jasmine and sandalwood are subtly combined with applications of natural yoghurt and a flower-scented bath to stimulate the senses and render the guest's skin velvet-smooth.

When the moon rises on the far side of the Ayung and casts its pale light over a jungle landscape alive with the characteristic sounds of the night, it is time to retreat to the sanctuary of one's own pavilion, where the silence is broken only by muffled sounds from the forest beyond and the occasional commotion of a flight of tropical birds.

Chiva-Som
Hua Hin, Thailand

The elegant pointed roofs of authentic Thai pavilions at the Chiva-Som Health Resort in the Bay of Hua Hin ('Haven of Life') are three hours and a million miles away from the capital, Bangkok. This prize-winning health and spa resort in the land of the Buddha is a shrine to meditation and contemplation.

The pavilions are scattered around an emerald lake, nestling in the fringes of the jungle or facing the variegated waters of the Gulf of Thailand. The interior decoration is simple yet uncommonly stylish, with local materials and only a sprinkling of items carved in wood to remind one that this is Asia: a statue of Buddha, perhaps, or a lamp base carved by a local artisan. There are no superfluous items and there is a complete absence of ostentation. In short, nothing to distract or disturb. Each pavilion has its own sala, a private, roofed lounge area which looks out over an exotic garden where the lightest of breezes carries the sweet and heady fragrances of tropical flowers and plants.

The Chiva-Som Spa is without equal in terms of its therapist staff and the range of treatments on offer. The Spa boasts no fewer than eighty qualified therapists who work in forty-five individual treatment suites and provide upwards of one hundred therapies and medical services. Each day begins with a meditation séance led by an aged Buddhist monk, freeing the mind to focus on essentials.

rural retreats

The essentials are encapsulated on a piece of parchment placed each night on every guest's bed: *Time is not an absolute. The underlying reality of all things is eternal. What we call 'time' is only a means to measure eternity.*

The holistic Chiva-Som approach to mind and body therapy strips away the bonds of 'civilisation' and all its social pressure and turns the mind in on itself in a process of self-discovery and self-knowledge. The sense of inner peace and well-being generated here is extremely rare – and attributable in large part to the dedication and diligence of resort personnel.

The night brings a muted symphony of birdsong, flapping wings and the soft cries emanating from the depths of the jungle beyond.

Interalpen-Hotel Tyrol
Telfs-Buchen, Austria

With spectacular mountain scenery all around, the Interalpen-Hotel lies in the snow-covered forests of the Seefeld Plateau some 1,300 metres high in the heart of the Austrian Alps. Well-known mountain peaks tower in the background and often the only sounds are those of the wind and the crunch of snow underfoot. The hotel lobby is dominated by an imperious carved wooden staircase and mezzanine, and is decked out with indoor fountains. Immense Venetian glass chandeliers cast a brilliant light. The walls are covered in Gobelin tapestries, the floors in precious oriental carpets and rugs. Chinese ornaments are dotted around the reception area. Beautiful wood panelling decorates the six interconnecting rooms of the *Stube*-style Tyrolean restaurant with its ornately-coffered ceiling. The chairs and tables are hand-carved both here and in the bedroom suites above. The suites are a honey-coloured symphony in wood, each with its own private terrace offering either a panorama of the picturesque Inn valley or a view of the imposing peaks of Karwendel and Wetterstein. A ceramic stove hints at romantic evenings by the fire and voluptuous eiderdowns promise a night of peaceful slumber.

The Interalpen Spa is as welcoming and comfortable as the hotel itself. The spa runs to 5,000 square metres, yet retains a sense of comfort and intimacy. Beauty treatments on offer range from massage to waxing and hydrotherapy. Saunas are housed in a village-like atmosphere of Tyrolean chalets and the guest can take a soothing walk along a shallow brook lined with rounded pebbles. The Crystal Bath is an oasis devoted to relaxation, a universe apart with softly tinkling crystal beads and light effects automatically triggered by changes in the acoustics. A 50-square-metre glass-walled pool is screened by conifers. Outside, hot tubs are available for relaxation in the crystalline air.

Hotel guests, weary after a tiring day on the slopes, typically opt to spend their evenings sitting snugly by the roaring log fire!

Les Prés d'Eugénie
Eugénie-les-Bains, France

Les Prés d'Eugénie is located between two thermal springs at Eugénie-les-Bains in the *département* of Les Landes. Today's hotel and restaurant complex brings together buildings dating back four hundred years: the Couvent aux Herbes, the Maison Rose, the Auberge de la Ferme aux Grives and La Ferme Thermale®. With its own unique charm each adds to the feeling of well-being achieved by combining tranquillity with luxury and style.

The Couvent aux Herbes ('Herbal Convent') cossets its guests in bedroom suites with log fires, splendid floor coverings, beautiful paintings and tenderly evocative names ('Minx', 'Rosa the Rose', 'Secret Garden' and so on). The Maison Rose ('The Pink House') is synonymous with country living at its most luxurious; here, white is the keynote colour on the ground floor, with sun yellow used for the interconnecting salons.

La Ferme aux Grives ('The Thrush Farm') is an mix of rusticity and elegance, with canopy beds and hollyhocks by the windows.

La Ferme Thermale® ('The Thermal Farm') is a haven of peace and tranquillity. There is no better phrase to describe this symphony of wood, marble and stone, with cotton fabrics enriched by pure wool and cashmere. Bath oils and druidic concoctions of aromatic and medicinal herbs perfume the air and assail the senses, while soothing water music ripples in the background.

The Imperial Cabin at La Ferme Thermale® is a traditional *boudoir*, bathed in light from morning to night and featuring a fireplace and a Louis XV easy chair.

A particular delight is to sink into the marble whirlpool bath and soak away life's stresses and strains, clearing the mind and revitalising the body by restoring its natural rhythms. Then it's time to relax in the Four Seasons garden, reclining in one of six curious 'wheelbarrow beds' which have been adapted from and inspired by an ancient Chinese design.

At night, the entire complex acquires a lyricism of its own and nothing compares with sitting in quiet contemplation of the starry heavens.

The Oberoi Rajvilas
Jaipur, Rajasthan, India

Rajasthan is a heady mix of exotic fragrances and explosive colours, a balm to the soul. Nowhere more so than in Jaipur, the Pink City, where astronomer-prince Bawai Man Singh built the fortress-like dream palace which is today one of the jewels in the crown of international hotel and resort group Oberoi.

A fortress outside, perhaps, but inside a fairy-tale tribute to the maharajahs. The hotel staff line up in full ceremonial dress to welcome the guest on arrival. The first impression is of opulence: impeccable furnishings, antiques, marble and stucco decor in the halls and dining room. The gardens are truly exceptional, an explosion of colour and fragrance, with fountains, a small lake and a temple. The floral theme is carried over into the bedrooms, bathrooms, lobby and reception. The luminous suites and tented rooms are the epitome of luxury: soft beige colours, embroidered fabric ceilings, ethereal drapes and colonial-style furniture. All elegance and refinement.

rural retreats

The Oberoi Rajvilas Spa, with its Banyan Tree logo, lives up to every expectation. This is no ordinary spa facility, it is a *sanctuary*. Flickering torches and waterspouts project subtle reflections on the walls. Fountains and small reflective ponds decorate the pool. Elevated kiosk-like cabins add to the overall feeling of intimacy. The spa achieves a perfect accord between oriental ritual and state-of-the-art sophistication and service.

One of the signature treatments here is – inevitably, perhaps – known as the Oberoi, a delicate massage duet performed in one of the spacious treatment cabins redolent of spices and ointments. The body is gently kneaded and pummelled to restore its latent energy and suppleness. The sensation of lightness is unforgettable.

Magical Indian evenings are spent under the stars with traditional dances and the distinctive notes of the *sarinda*.

ocean oases

Anassa
Polis, Cyprus

The road curves off into an abundance of lush vegetation and flowers, with aromas of jasmine and lavender. In the gentle light and shade of the Mediterranean, Anassa, the Queen of Cyprus, slowly reveals herself. Immaculately whitewashed two-storey villas with lavender-enamelled shutters and wrought-iron balconies. Elegantly furnished bedrooms and suites. Wisps of curtain and richly-textured bed linens. An ambience of pleasure and relaxation, pure and simple.

This magnificently Mediterranean setting, with its profusion of colours and plant life, would seem somehow incomplete if no provision were made to hone and condition the body. But provision *has* been made …

Anassa Spa offers a range of delights in its treatment cabins or tents erected on the fringe of the white sand beach, none more tempting than the herbal massage performed in the Roman Garden room under an azure sky. First comes a gentle head and foot massage to relax body and mind, followed by the application of fruit, plant and spice extracts and a full-body massage with firm and reassuring hands.

The skin starts to glow, the nerve ends begin to tingle. The sensations are voluptuous and exquisite.

Outside, there is no sound other than the rustle of the fountains, the occasional burst of birdsong and the whisper of a gentle breeze. And what better way to prolong this exceptional moment than to indulge in a glass of ice-cold champagne?

Banyan Tree Phuket
Thailand

Some destinations trigger a sense of anticipation at the mention of their name and Phuket belongs in this category. Manta rays and inoffensive sharks abound in the warm translucent waters of the Sea of Andaman, with its cathedral-like coral reefs.

The Banyan Tree Phuket takes its name from the venerable *banyan* tree native to Thailand. The resort complex is built on the site of an ancient mine — surely a shining example of environmental rehabilitation? — and is everything one could hope for in terms of taste and discreet luxury. The pointed roofs of the Lagoon Villas and the Spa Pool Villas are typical of traditional Thai architecture and thrust skywards through thickets of dense vegetation. This compromise between the natural and the man-made generates a subtle symbiosis between the human factor — the guest — and the surroundings. These guest villas are deployed around the lagoon and screened by bougainvillea, flamboyant frangipani trees and other sumptuous shrubs and blossoms. This exotic hideaway, with its Jim Thompson-designed silks, its lotus-flower pools, its tropical gardens, its teak floors and furniture, its carefully selected ornaments and its outsize beds, promotes an immediate sensation of well-being. The ultimate in luxury and romance, however, comes in the Spa Pool Villas. Each boasts its own private spa, a glass-walled infinity pool and, as if that were not enough, a candle-lit room built on wooden piles that appears to float on the water: the aptly-named Floating Bed Pavilion.

The Banyan Tree Spa offers dedicated spa facilities. This is undoubtedly the most famous spa facility in the whole of Asia — and justly so. Massage rooms are decorated with Buddha figurines and are complemented by sumptuous *salas*, small, roofed lounge areas (modelled on Thailand's royal palaces) open to the garden. Gold and green embroidered silks intensify the overall impression of seclusion and serenity.

Treatment is of the 'high-touch, low-tech' variety, with the emphasis on sensory stimulation and hands-on application of plant extracts and natural oils.

Among the plethora of treatments on offer, the Asian Blend massage is worthy of particular mention, adapted from traditional oil-free Thai massage techniques. Palms and thumbs are applied to identified pressure points in order to relieve tired muscles and improve circulation. Other options include the Thai Ginger Healer treatment (ginger root extract and yoga) or the Royal Banyan, which combines massage and full-body application of a citronella, coriander and sesame oil potion.

The Banyan Tree Spa is the epitome of romance, spirituality and communion with nature.

Cocoa Island
The Maldives

Cocoa Island is one of the spectacular string of small islands, like beads on a rosary, that form The Maldives. The stunning celadon greens and pale aniseed hues of the Indian Ocean set off the white-sand shorelines. The retreat is a forty-minute speedboat ride from Mali, capital of the Maldives, on a shimmering, mother-of-pearl island overlooking an emerald lagoon.

The bungalows are simple wooden beach houses, the design inspired by the *dhoni* boats used by local fishermen. These are dotted across the lagoon, like confetti, and combine to form a sort of weightless village floating in a cameo of rich turquoise, dark blue and indigo. Sting

rays and baby sharks frolic in the shallow aquamarine waters.

The guest bungalows are a back-to-nature experience, with fan palm latticework roofs, Zealand pine frames, generous bay windows, woven palm leaf ceilings and teak decking. Airy soft furnishings and furniture made by local artisans complete the picture.

The Como Shambhala Spa (*shambhala* is Sanskrit for 'peace') lives up to its name and adds a voluptuous final touch to the Cocoa Island experience. Deft hands apply essential oils as part of a range of Asian therapies and massage techniques in a setting that could scarcely be more exotic, given the pleasing combination of sea, sun and sand, and the delicious perfumes of hibiscus, ylang-ylang shrubs and wild sea-grape.

The signature Cocoa Island Bath is a full-body scrub with a dry brush followed by the application of a lotion based on macadamia nut oil, wheat bran flour and various essential oils to leave the skin satin-smooth. All this is rounded off with a therapeutic Ayurveda massage applied with both hands and feet. Tension and fatigue simply ebb away.

Relaxed evenings are spent beneath a soft tropical night-sky.

Domaine de Rochevilaine
Brittany, France

Amonumental 13th-century carved porch known as the Gate of Truth frames the entrance to the Domaine de la Rochevilaine on the Pointe de Pen Lan headland on the coast of Southern Brittany. The site so captivated the (admittedly somewhat eccentric) multi-millionaire Henri Dresch of Dresch motorbike fame that he decided to 'reconstitute' a Breton hamlet here.

That was back in the 1950s. Today, the Domaine de Rochevilaine hotel, restaurant and marine balneotherapy complex is a stunning evocation of a bygone Brittany, with its unique and mystic blend of *terre et mer*. The waves of the Atlantic Ocean break against the cliffs on which stands a *faux* yet authentic 'village' complete with an array of manor houses, a period-furnished château, fishermen's cottages and even a customs house. All are built from recycled granite blocks and each has broad expanses of windows and terraces overlooking the sea. The decor is inventive and, at times, whimsical: astrological signs, music scores, representations of the four seasons, the Seven Deadly Sins. Guests are housed in themed suites which evoke the ambience of the Orient or the post-modernism of a New York City loft or, indeed, the interior of a ship's cabin.

Once in the Aqua Phénicia hydrotherapy facility, time seems to stand still. The accent is on water and the revitalising properties of seaweed and sea salts. The signature Phoenician Table Treatment is based on documented massage techniques practised by the Phoenician explorers who ventured as far as the Breton coast two thousand years ago. The guest is ushered into a darkened room and invited to disrobe before submitting to sessions of herbal, hot stone and essential oil anti-stress therapy and massage. The entire experience cleanses the body and soothes the mind. It is – and there is no other term for it – akin to a quasi-religious ceremony.

Four Seasons Resort Bali
Jimbaran Bay

Lush terraces dotted with paddy fields stretch as far as the eye can see. A mother-of-pearl expanse of ocean glitters below. This other Eden is Jimbaran Bay, site of the exclusive Four Seasons Resort Bali.

Free-standing thatched-roofed pavilions cling to the slopes of the Bukit Permai hillside. Guestrooms, suites and villas open out on to a spacious terrace and a 200-metre-square swimming pool ringed by luxuriant plants and flowers, and redolent with exotic fragrances and essences. In the early morning, the air carries the distinctive fresh-sweet perfume which wafts from the frangipani trees. The view over Jimbaran Bay and towards Agung, Bali's sacred mountain, is, quite simply, breathtaking. A truly magical environment.

Time-honoured gesture and ritual pay homage to the body and celebrate the soul. Silken hands sooth away fatigue and stress. Indonesian *jamu* plant extract potions, handed down the generations from mother to daughter, are applied firmly and considerately.

At night, the resort is a Chinese shadow-play. With a Balinese moon reflected in a silver sea, myriad stars light up the heavens. Peace reigns.

Frégate Island Private
The Seychelles

Frégate Island Private is a miniscule resort located on a remote tropical island in the Seychelles. The island must rank as one of the most unspoilt places on earth. Seven attractively named beaches of purest white sand fringe the iridescent turquoise waters of the Indian Ocean. When a light shower falls, deliciously exotic fragrances are carried up from the surrounding jungle.

The island is a fragile ecosystem suspended between sky and sea. Sixteen luxury villas are scattered here and there on granite outcrops or amid the lush tropical vegetation, each designed to afford the discerning guest an unparalleled degree of privacy and comfort.

These superbly equipped yet simple post-and-lintel villas are built from traditional materials such as native mahogany, African teak and granite, and they are thatched with woven *ylang-ylang* palm leaves. The soft furnishings are predominantly linens and Thai-style Balinese silks.

The ultimate relaxation is to enjoy a therapeutic massage on your private terrace or to visit The Rock Spa. Treatments are based on water, fruit and plant extracts, essential oils and warm pebbles, but the possibilities are endless. Signature treatments include Sea Coconut Exfoliation (frangipani, vanilla and coconut) or a Zwazo Frégate – ninety minutes of sheer bliss. A Lekor Wrap is also a never-to-be-forgotten experience, where the body is treated with essential oils (papaya and mango) and wrapped in banana leaves.

The subtle interaction between Frégate Island's magnificent natural surroundings and the impeccably designed and beautifully decorated villa residences is at its most pronounced as night begins to fall and a pink glow filters through the jungle backdrop, spreading over terraces and woodwork.

Hotelito Desconocido
Tomatlan Jalisco, Mexico

The Hotelito Desconocido – literally, 'the unknown little hotel' – is situated on a natural wetland lagoon reserve known as Playton de Mismaloya, some sixty miles (but light years away) from the hustle and bustle that is Puerto Vallarta. The environmental reserve provides sanctuary for sea turtles, pink ibis, white jabiru storks and egrets.

The Hotelito's owner and developer, Marcello Murzilli, is immensely (and justifiably) proud of his 'eco-luxury' resort, the first such complex anywhere in the world operating *without* electricity. The Hotelito uses solar energy to power its air-conditioning units and other appliances; running water is channelled by wind-pump; and candlelight is *de rigueur* in the evening …

The bungalows – known locally as *palafitos* – are constructed on piles made of indigenous wood. Each has an ocean or a lagoon view. Diaphanous hand-woven mosquito nets make an afternoon siesta even more enjoyable. The walls are decorated in bold colours complementing the furniture and ornaments collected from Mexican haciendas. Narrow bridge walkways lead down to the lagoon, linking the individual bungalows and imparting a feeling of intimacy.

The Hotelito and the spa could scarcely be more romantic. The treatment rooms coil along the bank of a stream, open-sided to admit cooling sea breezes.

The mood is serene and authentic. Sophistication is not the watchword here. Instead, the accent is on communing with nature, feeling at one with the environment. The massage and therapy treatments in the El Mundo de la Salud spa are entrusted to qualified local masseurs; they firm and professional, without undue flamboyance. Abundant candles light up the Hotelito at night, bathing the complex in a warm, flickering glow. The waters of the lagoon gurgle gently in the background.

Katikies Suites
Santorini Island, Greece

The Katikies Suites are on Santorini, the volcanic Greek island with a legendary crater that helped create the legend of the Lost World of Atlantis. The resort complex balances like a tightrope-walker on the vertiginous black, ochre and red-striated cliff face which dominates the eponymous bay. It is an extraordinary concatenation of Cubist cottages silhouetted against an intensely blue sky. Architect Ilias Apostolidis was inspired by the ancient cliff dwellings of the Cyclades when he designed these spiral stairways, these hanging terraces and balconies, juxtaposings nooks and crannies which cling limpet-like to the rocks a hundred metres above the sea in defiance of the laws of gravity.

The meringue-like guestrooms with their whitewashed walls and vaulted ceilings have the essential simplicity that is the hallmark of resolutely contemporary design. The curtained walls and furniture are all a traditionally Greek virginal white, courtesy of leading interior decorator, Nikos Tzelepis. An immense infinity pool seems to merge with the sea, its surface tinged with sparkling reflections of the setting sun.

The Caldera Spa adopts a holistic approach. The terrace is lit by flickering candlelight and offers a magnificent panorama over Santorini Bay. Skilled hands knead and pummel the body, applying a special elixir of essential oils which penetrates deep into the lungs and satisfies the soul.

Stretched out on the masseur's table, the guest sees only a vast expanse of blue. At night, one can look over the parapet and revel in the absolute silence below, when even the waves seem sheet-metal still.

At moments like these, the Lost World of Atlantis seems invitingly close.

North Island
The Seychelles

This tiny granite island in the Seychelles archipelago is like a silver teardrop in the ocean, a short thirty-minute helicopter flight from the capital, Mahé. The entire island is a sanctuary, a one-off tribute to the spirit of romance and escapism.

The resort is a mini-kingdom of stones, pebbles, flax, roots and mother-of-pearl, a perfect marriage of light and shade, a harmonious blend of colours and natural materials, a sanctuary for flora and fauna. It is a place to reinvigorate the senses and replenish lost energies. On the immaculate beach, tasteful, coloured awnings flutter over wooden platforms and two immense mango trees offer additional shade. A few outsize and comfortable sunbeds lie in wait for nudist sun-worshippers.

The guest villas stretch along the beach or are tucked away in the Takamaka forest behind. Each has its own spectacular view. Each villa comprises two rooms and a private pool. Overhead, a ceiling fan turns quietly. The bathtub is fashioned from stone, the curtains are made from small pebbles, the accessories are in mother-of-pearl. The bay window areas are illuminated by a diffuse golden light from a meteorite-shaped lamp.

ocean oases

On the private terrace, guests can indulge in a signature massage – the aromatic ESPA, based on sea salts and essential oils – while gazing down on the marine life below. Contemplating this underwater ballet while succumbing to the soporific to-and-fro of skilled hands gently caressing one's oiled body dispels all notions of time and space and induces a trance-like state of pure and utter well-being.

The soft rays of the setting sun filter through the giant leaves of fan palms against the backdrop of a stormy sky.

Parrot Cay
Turks and Caicos

A languid sun sinks slowly into the Caribbean … set back from the churning waves that pound the coral reef, the villas of the Parrot Cay Resort are like many sea-birds poised to take to the air. Or giant white water lilies spread open on a sea of dazzling white sand or a lush tropical garden. This is a truly wild Eden, with mangrove swamps, frangipani trees and cacti plants home to more than seventy-five species of birdlife ranging from flamingos to red-breasted hummingbirds.

The tiny resort of Parrot Cay in the Turks and Caicos archipelago is the brainchild of Como Hotels owner Christina Ong. It is a top-of-the-range sanctuary for the rich and privileged, an exceptional resort where no effort has been spared to create an oasis of tranquillity. The plantation-like villas and guest suites are cooled by fresh sea-breezes. Here, the fundamentals of *feng shui* are not only respected but interpreted with flair and elegance. Canopy beds harmonise with the painted walls, the pure white bed linen and soft furnishings, the dark teak furniture and the rush matting floors. Colonial-style ceiling fans whir overhead. The bathroom suites are equally delightful, with wooden parquet floors and an adjoining patio with a shower unit installed against a stone wall.

The Como Shambhala Spa nestles on a hillside amid tropical plants and shrubs, exuding the fragrances of exotic flowers and rare essences. Everything here is so inviting, so authentic. Pampered guests readily submit to daily ministrations, including expert traditional massages, anointment with precious oils and floral and plant extracts, and seaweed and herbal wraps that leave the skin velvet-smooth. The calm is broken only by the mellow touch of a gentle breeze and the muted thunder of the ocean beyond.

There is no spectacle to match the flamboyance of a Caribbean sun setting in a blaze of red and gold.

Le Prince Maurice
Belle Mare, Mauritius

Mauritius is an island of dreams set in the Mascareignes archipelago, and is truly a pearl of the Indian Ocean. Mauritius is also home to Le Prince Maurice, a resort dedicated to the art of tropical living, a secret hideaway promising romance and exoticism.

The entrance hall is tapered like a cathedral nave. Flower-ringed pools stretch out towards the distant lagoon and intensify the overall sense of luxury and sensuality. The decor is resolutely *feng shui*, impeccably understated, quietly luxurious, with furniture and ornaments placed subtly here and there. Hints of frangipani, ylang-ylang and vanilla perfume the air. The guest suites, set amid lush tropical vegetation or on stilts along the shore, are warm and inviting, with chestnut-coloured parquet floors, cushions and soft furnishings in muted colours, and the signature fragrance of nutmeg.

ocean oases

A palm-lined walkway leads to the prestigious Guerlain Institute Spa, with its pagoda roofs, waxed floors in dark wood, orange lanterns, ubiquitous water features and Balinese-style roofless treatment rooms. The decor is pleasingly exotic: this is a temple for the initiated. Treatments here include a superb four-handed massage (a rhythmic duet on sun-drenched skin) followed by an invigorating shower in the small indoor courtyard. The calm is punctuated only by the soft whispering of the sea.

The dawn of each new day is greeted by cheerful birdsong at first light.

Royal Malewane
Hoedspruit, South Africa

The Royal Malewane Luxury Safari Lodge lies on the western fringes of the greater Kruger National Park. Here, in southern Africa's 'Big Five' territory, the wide, open, unspoilt spaces of Africa beckon.

The Royal Malewane accommodates a maximum number of sixteen guests at any one time, in six free-standing private suites that look out over the bushveld, each with its rich dark wood terrace, thatched gazebo and private pool. Elevated wooden walkways link the guest suites to the richly furnished and carpeted main resort building with its library, shop, dining and lounge areas. The suite interiors are ruggedly colonial and neo-classical in style, with an air-conditioned bedroom/sitting room, an open fireplace for chilly nights, antique furniture and a king-size canopy bed with Ralph Lauren bed linen. Beautifully appointed bathrooms feature lion's foot Victorian bathtubs and indoor and outdoor showers. In short, every possible comfort after a tiring day on safari.

The same mood prevails in the Royal Malewane gym and spa, designed to harmonise with the lodge's natural surroundings. Two internationally-trained therapists are on hand to provide a range of massage, aromatherapy, hydrotherapy and skincare treatments. These can be enjoyed on a secluded terrace, in a roofed open-sided *sala* nestling amid the acacia thorns, in a glass-walled bungalow with views across the surrounding terrain or, if preferred, in the privacy of the guest suites.

The palatial spa bath boasts a bird's-eye view over the bush. From this vantage point, guests can lie back and relax, watching impala drink at the watering-hole and keeping an eye open for the occasional elephant.

The Royal Malewane is a unique and exclusive destination for those who value style and personalised service – not to mention some of the best game viewing Africa has to offer. The evenings are a particular delight, relaxing on the terrace, taking in the fresh and invigorating bushveld air and the sights and sounds of the wild.

The feelings of solitude and sense of space offered here are unrivalled.

Taha'a Pearl Beach Resort and Spa
French Polynesia

The Polynesian Islands are synonymous in most people's minds with dazzling sunlight, beautifully transparent lagoons of shimmering turquoise, and silver-flecked waves breaking on a mother-of-pearl beach. These images, clichéd as they may be, are nonetheless firmly anchored in reality.

The Taha'a Private Island Resort and Spa is superbly located on the coral islet of Motu Tautau, not far from Raiatea. It faces the island of Taha'a on the lagoon side and the island of Bora Bora on the ocean side.

The irresistibly romantic villas are dotted amid lush vegetation or perched on stilts (Over-Water Suites). For all their Robinson Crusoe-like appearance, however, these 'huts' are anything but primitive. With their *pandanu* (woven palm frond) roofs, their wooden frames, braided rope walls and ochre-coloured Taha'a stone features, they are not only perfectly integrated into their natural surroundings but also pay tribute to local craftsmanship. The suites, with their large bay windows, offer a panoramic view of a timeless ocean beyond.

The Manea Spa lies in the shade of a coconut grove between the meandering waters of a small lake and the turquoise lagoon. The heady scent of ylang-ylang and Tahitian *tiare* (a variety of gardenia) mixes with more subtle fragrances of frangipani and jasmine. The smell of vanilla, the black gold of Polynesia, is unmistakable but is tempered by notes of sandalwood, coconut, pineapple and *tamanu* (poon). These and other natural products are all central to Polynesian *Taurumi* philosophy which regards the act and art of massage as an integral component of everyday life.

Qualified Taha'a Resort therapists gently massage the body with pineapple-extract lotions such as Monoï Païnapo or Païnapo Manea. (Pineapple has valuable cosmetic properties as a moisturising agent.) The ultimate finishing touch comes in the form of a banana leaf body wrap, which leaves the skin soft and supple.

And what better way to end the day than a hand-in-hand barefoot walk by moonlight along the deserted beach?

Taj Exotica Resort and Spa
Flic en Flac, Mauritius

The blue darkens and becomes more intense as the Indian Ocean shelves towards the horizon. On land, vast expanses of sugar cane form another sea, this time a swaying mass of green. We are on the island of Mauritius once more, this time at the Taj Exotica Resort and Spa, a twenty-seven acre haven of peace and solitude overlooking the serene waters of Tamarin Bay.

Colonial Mauritian architecture is the watchword for the sixty-five elegant villas and suites that make up the Taj Exotic Resort, a flagship getaway destination belonging to the Taj Group. Interiors are decidedly contemporary, a hybrid of African, Asian and Arabic influences, with distinctly Indian design features in the guestrooms, bathrooms and reception areas.

The outside patio has a shower and a secluded plunge pool area complete with oriental lamp fittings and generously proportioned sofas with muted cream cushions. The view from the terrace extends all the way to the horizon. A fawn and ivory pebble walkway rings the sunken bath. Precious wood, stone and wrought-iron objects are scattered here and there. Chocolate-colour daybeds with yellow scatter cushions are set out on a teak deck. An infinity pool adds another exotic note. In the background, intimate beach huts invite young lovers to spend some lingering moments together.

The Taj Spa is customised to instil a sense of spiritual and physical release. As one enters, a thousand tiny details catch the eye and proclaim the mystery and mystique that is India. Midnight-blue daybeds are arranged next to reflecting pools. Tiny bells tinkle magically in the background. Beaten copper bowls are filled with purifying water. Everything, even down to the sandalwood 'third eye' applied out of respect for the gods, is steeped in Ayurvedic philosophy, including the names applied to the individual treatments: Samattva, Sushupti, Vishrama. A feeling of intoxication and intense well-being sets in as silky hands ritually massage the body with exotic oils and essences. The sensual ritual is completed with a garland of Ginda flowers. Synonymous with understated elegance and impeccable hospitality, The Taj Exotica Resort and Spa fully lives up to its name.

The Chedi Muscat
Sultanate of Oman

The Sultanate of Oman, the sun-drenched peninsula that separates the Persian Gulf from the Gulf of Oman, is one of the last remaining authentic examples of traditional Arab society. The town of Muscat, situated in the heart of mysterious Arabia, dates from the first century AD. Here, the sun's glare sun reflects back from the crystal waters of the Gulf of Oman and the dry-earth buildings that fringe the ocean, prompting author Pierre Loti, who chanced upon this place in 1900, to describe the steep Haajjar mountains beyond this isolated city as 'rising wall-like from the blue waters of the bay'.

The traditional arches, domes, high narrow windows and mother-of-pearl white façades of the Chedi Muscat owe their clean lines and exotic, yet understated, design to the vision of architect Jean-Michel Gathy. The entire complex has a geometrical purity that is eminently contemporary and yet is imbued with a sense of serenity and ageless Arabic charm.

The guestrooms and suites have dark floors and stylish wooden furniture and panelling set off by cream and sand-coloured walls, sofas and soft furnishings. This symmetrical, minimalist approach is continued into the spa facility, where perspectives and materials immediately immerse the guest in a serene and unobtrusive Zen-like atmosphere underpinned by soft music and a simple, yet chic, decor. The aromatherapy massage is a return to basics, a treatment to restore body and mind. Herb and plant extract-based essential oils induce a sense of well-being and utter relaxation that anticipates the ultimate pleasure lying ahead: sitting in quiet contemplation as the dark-blue of the night sky merges into the immensity of the ocean.

The Twelve Apostles
Cape Town, South Africa

A shimmering white-sand beach fringed with shrubs rustling in a soft sea breeze. The muffled roar of Atlantic rollers rushing over the reef. And, in the near distance, the silent sentinels of the Cape: the majestic Table Mountain and the imposing Twelve Apostles range.

Set against this stunning backdrop is the luxury Twelve Apostles Hotel complex, a hedonist's heaven a stone's throw from Cape Town. Traditional Dutch scroll architecture and modern styling combine to impart a distinctly contemporary, yet timeless, atmosphere. Some of the guestrooms and suites, set in four secluded wings linked to the public areas via airy walkways, adopt a marine theme with shell and fish motifs, while others draw inspiration directly from the African bush that lies beyond.

ocean oases

The 12A Sanctuary Spa is a holistic universe dedicated to the healing power and purity of nature and the surrounding elements of earth, sea and sky. It is a quiet, peaceful place, except for the relaxing sound of water trickling through pools set into a natural grotto, and it also offers man-made features such as a Hydro Pool, the Brine Pool or a hot-and-cold Plunge Pool.

The signature treatments here are invigorating massages and wraps using indigenous plant extracts. There are other treatments based on rare essences from the Clarins' International Spa Range.

The Spa health bar, with its rich, dark mahogany tables and custom-built units, was designed by the Cape's exciting new interior architect, Gregg Mellor.

Zimbali Lodge
South Africa

The Zimbali Lodge ('Place of Flowers' in Zulu) is an exclusive hideaway resort on the Dolphin Coast Forest Reserve some thirty miles from Durban on South Africa's east coast. This is a three hundred-hectare sub-tropical paradise of extraordinary and unspoilt natural beauty with immaculate white-sand beaches that seem to stretch on forever.

The Lodge directly overlooks the Indian Ocean beach and is surrounded by lush vegetation and manicured indigenous gardens. Much of its innate charm can be attributed to the estate architecture, which is an effective mixture of colonial turn-of-the-century styling and local design and craftsmanship.

Guestrooms and suites are scattered about the resort in the form of individual lodges whose timeless elegance is a tribute to the skills of interior designers Wilson & Associates (whose other credits include the Lost City complex at Sun City and Cape Town's Table Bay Hotel). Carved mahogany beds with mosquito nets and delicately ornate furniture. Decorative wall panelling, scatter rugs and floors stained dark brown. Luxurious bathrooms feature *fin-de-siècle* pewter fittings, wrought-iron lamps and Victorian bathtubs. Balconies that overlook the lake, the forest and the ocean beyond are visited by the occasional uninvited, but welcome, guests such as monkeys, crested and long-tailed *turacos* and *bulbul* songbirds.

The Zimbali Lodge Health and Beauty Spa also has a colonial style. Guests succumb to simple treatments and therapies featuring essential oils and relaxing massage therapy. Gentle hands massage away everyday aches and pains and soothe the mind. Relaxation is the watchword in this unique cocoon nestling amid exotic vegetation and lulled by the mysterious sounds of the African jungle.

Towards evening, the light softens and dims. Another page in the history of this wild continent has been written. But the dream lingers ...

contact information

Anassa
P.O. Box 66006
8830 Polis
Cyprus
Tel: (357) 26 888 000
Fax: (357) 26 322 900
Email: res.anassa@thanoshotels.com
www.thanoshotels.com

Banyan Tree Phuket
33 Moo 4, Srisoonthorn Road
Cherngtalay, Amphur Talang
Phuket 83110
Thailand
Tel: (66) 76 324 374
Fax: (66) 76 271 463
Email: phuket@banyantree.com
www.banyantree.com

Les Barmes de l'Ours
Chemin des Carats
73150 Val-d'Isère
France
Tel: (33) [0] 4 79 41 37 00
Fax: (33) [0] 4 79 41 37 01
www.hotel-les-barmes.com

Begawan Giri Estate
P.O. Box 54
Ubud 80571
Bali
Indonesia
Phone: (62) 361 978 888
Fax: (62) 361 978 889
Email: reservations@begawan.com
www.begawan.com

The Chedi Muscat
North Ghubra 232, Way n° 3215, Street n° 46
Muscat
Sultanate of Oman
Postal address:
P.O. Box 964
133, Al Khuwair
Muscat
Sultanate of Oman
Tel: (968) 24 52 44 00
Fax: (968) 24 49 34 85 or (968) 24 49 44 86
Email: chedimuscat@ghmhotels.com
www.ghmhotels.com

Chiva-Som
Hua Hin
73/4 Petchkasem Road
Hua Hin, Prachuab Khirikhan 77110
Thailand
Tel: (66) [0] 3253 6536
Fax: (66) [0] 3251 1154
Email: reservation@chivasom.com
www.chivasom.com

Cocoa Island (Como Hotels and Resorts)
Makunifushi
South Malé Atoll
The Maldives
Tel: (960) 441818
Fax: (960) 441919
Email: sales@cocoisland.como.bz
www.cocoa-island.com

Domaine de Rochevilaine
Pointe de Pen Lan
56190 Billiers
France
Tel: (33) [0] 2 97 41 61 61
Fax: (33) [0] 2 97 41 44 85
Email: domaine@domainerochevilaine.com
www.domainerochevilaine.com

Four Seasons Hotel George V Paris
31, avenue George-V
75008 Paris
France
Tel: (33) [0] 1 49 52 70 00
Fax: (33) [0] 1 49 52 70 10
www.fourseasons.com

Four Seasons Hotel Ritz Lisbon
Rua Rodrigo da Fonseca, 88
Lisbon, Portugal 1099-039
Tel: (351) 21 381-1400
Fax: (351) 21 383-1783
www.fourseasons.com

Four Seasons Resort Bali at Jimbaran Bay
Jimbaran, Denpasar
80361 Bali
Indonesia
Tel: (62) 361 701 010
Fax: (62) 361 701 020
www.fourseasons.com

Frégate Island Private
P.O. Box 330
Victoria
Mahé
Republique of the Seychelles
Tel: (248) 282 282
www.fregate.com

Gran Hotel La Florida
Carretera Vallvidrera Al Tibidabo 83-93
08035 Barcelona
Spain
Tel: (34) 93 259 30 00
Fax: (34) 93 259 30 01
Email: reservation@hotellaflorida.com
www.hotellaflorida.com

Hotelito Desconocido
Playon de Mismaloya Sin Numero
La Cruz de Loreto
Tomatlan Jalisco
Mexico
Postal address: Hotelito Desconocido
Apartado Postal 2-14
Puerto Vallarta, Jalisco
ZIP 48350
Mexico
Tel: (52) 322 281 4010
Fax: (52) 322 281 4130
Email: hotelito@hotelito.com
www.hotelito.com

Interalpen-Hotel Tyrol
Dr-Hans-Liebherr-Alpenstraße 1
6410 Telfs-Buchen
Austria
Tel: (43) 5262 606 0
Fax: (43) 5262 606 190
Reservations: (43) 5262 606 281
Email: interalpen@interalpen.com
www.interalpen.com

Katikies Suites
Oia
Santorini 84702
Cyclades Islands
Greece
Tel: (30) 22860 71214
Fax: (30) 22860 71312
Email: info@katikies.com
www.katikies.com

Ksar Char-Bagh
Palmeraie de Marrakech
40000 Marrakech
Morocco
Tel: (212) 4 43 29 24
www.ksarcharbagh.com

Mandarin Oriental Hyde Park
66 Knightsbridge
London SW1X 7LA
UK
Tel: (44) [0] 207 201 3773
Fax: (44) [0] 207 201 3703
Email: molon-info@mohg.com
www.mandarinoriental.com

Mandarin Oriental New York
80 Columbus Circle at 60th Street
New York, NY 10023
USA
Tel: (1) 212 805 8800
Fax: (1) 212 805 8888
Email: monyc-reservations@mohg.com
www.mandarinoriental.com

North Island Seychelles
P.O. Box 1176
Victoria
Mahé
Republic of the Seychelles
Tel: (248) 293 100
Fax: (248) 293 150
Email: info@north-island.com
www.north-island.com
www.northislandspa.com

The Oberoi Rajvilas
Goner Road
Jaipur, Rajasthan 303 012
India
Tel: (91) 141 268 0101
Fax: (91) 141 268 0202
Email: gm@oberoi-rajvilas. com
www.oberoihotels.com or www.
oberoirajvilas.com

Parrot Cay
P.O. Box 164
Providenciales
Turks and Caicos Islands
British West Indies
Tel: (1) 649 946 7788
Fax: (1) 649 946 7789
Email: res@parrotcay.como.bz
www.besthotelsresorts.com

Les Prés d'Eugénie
40320 Eugénie-les-Bains
France
Tel: (33) [0] 5 58 05 06 07
Fax: (33) [0] 5 58 51 10 10
Email: reservation@michelguerard.com
www.michelguerard.com

Le Prince Maurice
Poste de Flacq
Belle Mare
Mauritius
Tel: (230) 413 9100
Fax: (230) 413 9130 or (230) 413 9129
Email: resa@princemaurice.com
www.princemaurice.com or www.
constancehotels.com

La Réserve
301, route de Lausanne
1293 Bellevue
Geneva
Switzerland
Tel: (41) 22 959 59 59
Email: info@lareserve.ch or
reservation@lareserve.ch or
soa@lareserve.ch
www.lareserve.ch

Royal Malewane
P.O. Box 1542
Hoedspruit 1380
South Africa
Tel: (27) [0] 15 793 0150
Fax: (27) [0] 15 793 2879
Email: info@royalmalewane.com
or reservation@royalmalewane.com
www.royalmalewane.com

The Setai
2001 Collins Avenue
Miami
Florida 33139
USA
Tel: (1) 305 520 6000
Fax: (1) 305 520 6111
Email: setai@ghmhotels.com
www.setai.com

Taha'a Pearl Beach Resort and Spa
BP 67 Patio Taha A
French Polynesia/Polynésie française 98733
Tel: (689) 608 400
Email: infos@letahaa.com or
letahaa@relaischateaux.com
www.letahaa.com

Taj Exotica Resort and Spa
Wolmar, Flic en Flac
Mauritius
Tel: (230) 403 1500
Fax: (230) 453 5555
Email: exotica.mauritius@tajhotels.com
www.tajhotels.com

The Twelve Apostles
P.O. Box 32117
Camps Bay 8040
Cape Town
South Africa
Tel: (27) [0] 21 437 9000
Fax: (27) [0] 21 437 9001
Email: bookta@rchmail.com
www.12apostleshotel.com
www.redcarnationhotels.com

Zimbali Lodge
P.O. Box 404
Umhali
Zimbali 4390
South Africa
Tel: (27) 15871 4053
www.suninternational.com

photographic credits

Marc Charuel 48-49 b, 58 b, 59.

Corbis *Casa Productions* 60-61 – *Craig Tuttle* 36-37 – *Charles O'Rear* 8-9.

Pierre Hausherr cover 2, 10 r, 11, 12, 13, 76 to 79, 94 to 97, 104 to 107.

Ludovic Maisant 1, 26-27, 62, 63, 80 to 83, 108, 109.

acknowledgements

The editor would like to thank the following for their assistance:

Banyan Tree Phuket 64 to 67 – **Les Barmes de l'Ours** 4 (1), 5 (4), 38 to 41 – **Begawan Giri Estate** 4 (5), 42 to 45 – **Chiva-Som** 5 (5), 46, 47, 48 l, 48-49 t, 49 r – **Cocoa Island** 4 (6), 68, 69 – **Domaine de Rochevilaine** 4 (4), 70 to 73 – **Four Seasons Hotel George V Paris** 101 – **Four Seasons Hotel Ritz Lisbon** 4 (3), 5 (1), 14 to 17 – **Four Seasons Resort Bali** 74, 75 – **Gran Hotel La Florida** 4 (2), 18 to 21 – **Interalpen-Hotel Tyrol** 4-5, 6, 6-7, 50, 51, 116-117, 118-119 – **Katikies Suites** cover 4, 84 to 87 – **Ksar Char-Bagh** 5 (2), 22 to 25 – **Mandarin Oriental** 28, 29 – **North Island** cover 1 (©Wilderness Safaris), cover 3 (© Michael Poliza), 88, 89 t (© Michael Poliza), 89 bl, 89 br, 90, 91 (©Wilderness Safaris) – **The Oberoi Rajvilas** 56-57, 58 t – **Parrot Cay** 92, 93 – **Les Prés d'Eugénie** 5 (6), 52 to 55 – **La Réserve** 30, 31 – **Royal Malewane** 98 to 101 – **The Setai** 32 to 35 – **Taha'a Pearl Beach Resort and Spa** 5 (3), 102, 103 – **The Twelve Apostles** 110 to 113 – **Zimbali Lodge** 114, 115.

And also:
Anassa, The Chedi Muscat, Frégate Island Private, Mandarin Oriental Hyde Park, Hotelito Desconocido, Le Prince Maurice, Taj Exotica Resort and Spa.